Ada Learns to Sew

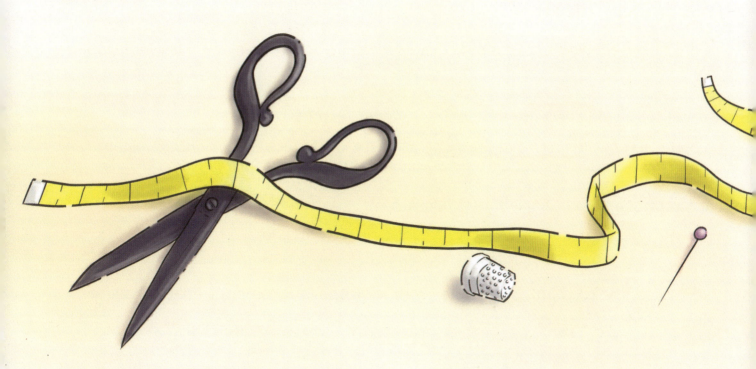

Publishing Data

First edition published 2023 (SSCB01)
Copyright Angie Scarr
Illustrations Scott Macniven
Design by Frank Fisher
Sliding Scale, Plaza De Andalucía 1, Campofrío, 21668, Huelva, Spain.

ISBN 979-8864288641

All rights reserved. No part of this book may be reproduced, or transmitted in any form or by any means without the express permission of the copyright owners.

The right of Angie Scarr to be identified as the author of this work has been asserted in accordance with the Copyright Designs and Patents Act 1988, sections 77 & 78.

No part of this publication may be reproduced, stored in a retrieval system or transmitted in any form or by any means without the prior permission of the publisher and author or their agents.

For information about Angie's craft books etc.
www.angiescarr.com

We would like to thank Stephanie Ryan for generous support enabling us to complete this project.

Ada is in a mood.
Her dark eyes always show when she's grumpy. She tosses a curl out of her eyes and tells her mum no, she doesn't want to put on her coat and take the dog for a walk. Today she has decided she wants to sit and think. Ada likes to think. She stares out of her bedroom window at the heavy raindrops splashing several centimetres off the pavement. She's just finished a phone call with her nanny but she was grumpy even then. Nanny was always chattering away, asking what she was doing, but she wasn't doing anything. It was raining and she didn't want to go out, that's all.

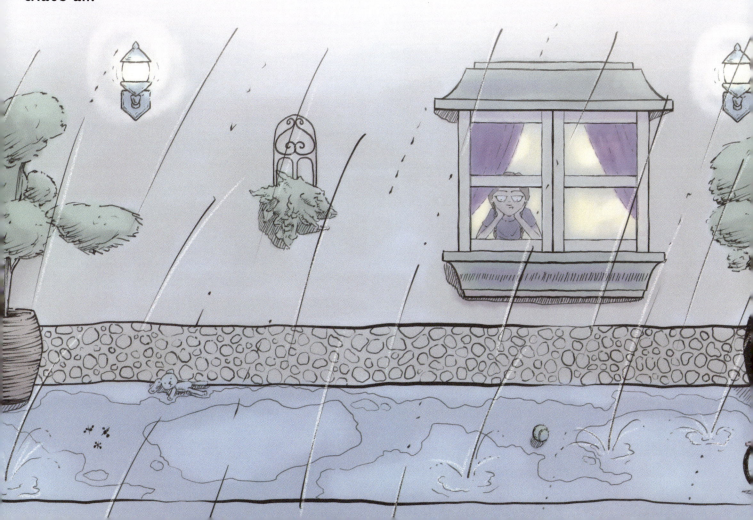

Nanny just laughed at her and Ada tried not to laugh at herself too. She didn't want to be cheered up. She liked being grumpy. Sometimes, she caught sight of herself in the mirror when she was grumpy, and she thought she looked strange and she giggled just a little in spite of herself. First, all intense scowling eyes, then suddenly the sunny-day Ada that was always inside, but she didn't always want to show. Today she wanted to be fierce like the tigers on her play mat or cheeky like the monkey hanging from her bedside lamp. She wanted to have a long memory like her stuffed elephant or like Great Grandma Christine, who Ada thought must remember when the world started and everywhere was jungle. And everyone was called old-fashioned names.

Some people called Ada 'older than her years'. They said things like 'she's been here before', and once her Nanny had even told her that her name was very, very old, like a musty handkerchief or an ancient perfume bottle without any perfume in it. The name had belonged to her great great great… maybe Nanny said four greats, but Ada lost count.

Some kind of grandma who lived in the olden days but wasn't alive now. Nanny said "I knew her when I was a girl and she was very old then," like that was ever possible. "When I was a girl just like you," Nanny used to say. It sounded weird. Nanny was Nanny. Wrinkly and old and sometimes, Dad said, 'a bit odd'.

Sometimes Nanny would say "I'm only 20 years older than your Dad!" as if that wasn't much. But 20 was like Auntie Kira's brother Teo… and that was old too. Ada couldn't imagine being that old, but maybe she would be one day. She put on the little pearl necklace Nanny had given her when she had told her about Mummy and Daddy's wedding in Thailand. Ada did a twirl like she imagined a lady of 20 would. Yes. She could imagine being 20. She rather liked the sound of it. 'Happy 20th birthday, Ada!' But it was a long time away.

She put the necklace back in the box that said 'Pretty Old Things', where she'd written it just after her sixth birthday. She remembered writing it even though it was ages ago and her writing was better now she was six and a half. "Ada is six and a half" she said to herself. And people said that was old. But not as old as great great whaterveritwas Ada, who she imagined must have been another old pretty thing because it was her box that Nanny had given to Ada on her sixth birthday when everyone else was giving her fairies because fairies are what she liked. But they didn't know that it wasn't so much pink plastic Barbies with butterfly wings that she liked.

Ada liked real fairies. She liked the idea of being a fairy. Not a bright plasticky fairy with a sticky-out skirt but a proper wispy fairy you could see right through. But people laughed at her when she said that, because they said fairies weren't real. Well, Grandma said they might be but you would never see one because they were quick and they lived at the bottom of the garden and didn't like people. Grandad said "Hey, why don't we go and look for fairies" and they looked for a whole hour but there weren't any fairies, even though Grandad had pulled up weeds to look under them. Grandad said "They're very shy, like foxes", and he pointed to some marks in the garden that he said were fox footprints. When she started to cry, he told her foxes didn't eat fairies just bird food and old bits of bread.

Once when she'd been with Nanny and Grandad Flan at the fuente where Flan got the drinking water, she was certain she'd seen two fairies dancing. One in bright red and one in turquoise and green glittery dresses. She'd cried out and jumped out of the car to try and catch one as it danced away through the weeds and watercress. Nanny laughed when she told her and said they must have been dragonflies which liked dancing around the damp hollow where the river Odiel started. The way Grandad Flan said Oh-dee-el it sounded smelly like odious but it wasn't. The water was sweet and cool and the animals liked it because Flan had pointed out a little turtle hiding in the watercress. It didn't look anything like the mutant turtles. Or even Ada's finger puppet turtle. It was sort of darker and more shy and hidey.

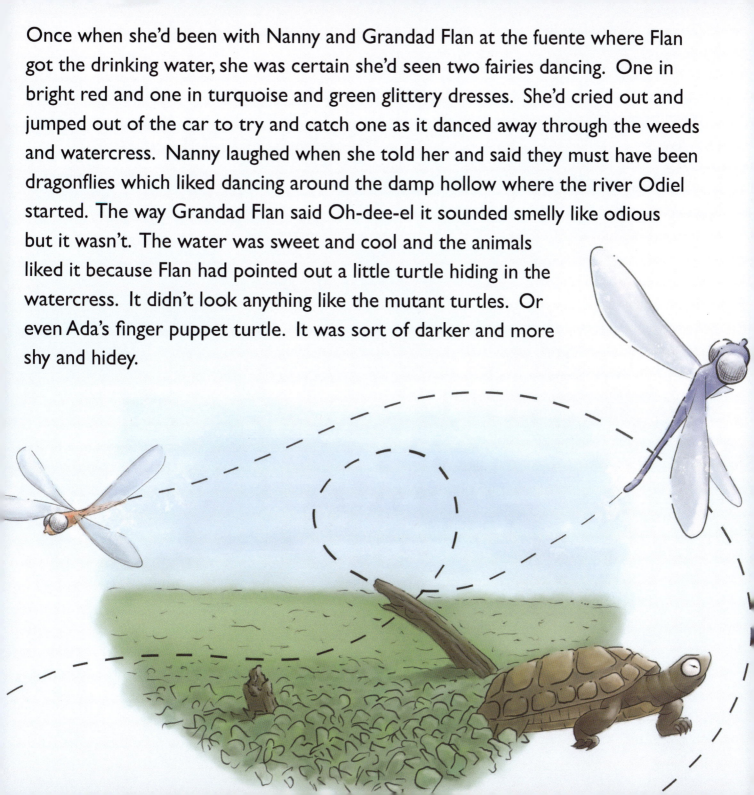

Ada liked that she'd be able to tell Becca that there were real turtles and real fairies in Spain. But she knew Becca wouldn't believe her. Nanny said that her name was pronounced AhDah in Spanish and that sounded like the Spanish word hada, which means fairy, so she thought she might tell Becca that she'd turned into a fairy too, but then she knew that would sound silly back in West Yorkshire where fairies hid at the bottom of gardens. In Spain, fairies were cheeky and danced around right in front of your eyes!

Somehow, Ada didn't mind Nanny laughing at her because that's what Nanny always did. Her and Flan were always teasing people, but when Ada looked at those wrinkly laughing eyes, Nanny sometimes winked as if they were sharing a secret joke. Nanny even laughed at Daddy sometimes and you could tell Daddy didn't like it. Nanny called Daddy her 'little boy'. Ada wondered why she did that. Daddy would sigh and say 'that's just what she does.' She called Auntie Kira 'my little girl' too once, and she was sure Nanny often had a tear in her eye when she said that kind of thing, but when Ada asked her, she said she wasn't sad. Ada liked hearing this because she cried a lot too, and sometimes she wasn't even sad and wasn't quite sure why she was crying. Sometimes she was frustrated with the shoelaces on her school shoes and wanted to wear her trainers with the Velcro instead and sometimes she was just in a mood for no reason; like today.

Nanny always told stories about things that had made her happy or sad or just stories of things that had happened when she was a little girl. Ada wasn't sure which ones were true and which weren't, but when she asked, Nanny would just open her eyes as wide as possible, maybe even wider than that, and say "of course, it's all true darling. " And Ada knew it was, unless there was that wink, and then she knew maybe a little bit of it was just made up, for fun. Like the time she said she turned Auntie Kira into a ladybird just 'cos she was crying. Then she gave her the biggest wink and she knew it wasn't really true. Later Auntie Kira told her she actually did turn her into a ladybird but it was just dressing up for insect day at school, and she did it by sewing her a costume with wings, with big black spots on and insect feelers in her hair.

Ada sat pressing her nose repeatedly on the window, watching it make little nose marks on the shiny glass. Mummy had taken the dog out without her and Uncle Ollie was at their house helping Wren with his counting. Wren liked counting. He could count even better than Ada and he was only in Mr Hogarth's class! Uncle Ollie knew everything about counting. And he knew everything about computers, And he and Uncle Alan sometimes talked in funny words that they said were about how computers think.

Grandad Flan knew about computers as well, but Flan shouted at Daddy's computer a lot and said it had windows that didn't work. Ada couldn't see any windows, and thought Flan must be talking rubbish. But Nanny said Flan knew about computers and her eyes weren't even wide open. She just said it, like it was true.

She looked at her box of pretty old things and couldn't remember if she'd written 'Pretty Old' as in 'a little bit ancient' or if she had wanted to say the things were both pretty and old. Ada liked English class better than maths. Mrs Goodwin read stories like she was taking you there with her. When she told the one about the little men who lived on a toy boat and ate peppermint creams, you could nearly-really taste the peppermint! Maths was hard and boring and you couldn't see pictures in your head when you were writing numbers. Well, except for if you stared really hard and the number 4 turned into a chair and the number 3 was a chicken and 2 was always a swan, because she remembered that the 2 was a swan on the wall when she was in preschool.

She remembered the birthday when she got the box. She didn't know if she was dreaming or not because when she tried to open her eyes they were stuck together and Mum and Dad and Wren were singing Happy Birthday, but they looked like aliens silhouetted against the early morning light that streamed through the window. "I can't see!" she screamed. "I've gone blind." And Mummy and Daddy took her, wrapped in her blanket, straight to the health centre where the nice lady (she knew she was nice because Mummy kept telling her that she was going to see the nice doctor) had looked into her eyes and her ears and even asked her very loudly to say ahh, even though she could hear very well and just couldn't see her properly.

Then she told Mummy to get some eye cream and pressed some paper into Ada's hand. And said 'happy birthday.'

"Say thank you," said Mummy, and Ada remembered saying thank you very quietly, although she didn't know what for. When they got to the chemist shop the lady there said "what's the matter?" and Mummy said it was Ada's birthday and she didn't have to go to school because she couldn't see properly. And the lady sucked her teeth just like Nanny sometimes did and said "poor wee mite" and came out from behind the counter and pressed a soft toy bunny into her armpit. Which seemed a bit strange.

Mummy said the bunny had a bunch of flowers and a headband but she couldn't see it properly except that the headband was pink. And the flowers were really tiny. Ada had never seen, or felt, such tiny flowers before. Then she went home and Wren helped her to open her presents. Mummy opened Nanny's present to her and said it was a bit of a weird and old-fashioned thing to give to a six year old. Dad said "Well, what do you expect from Mum?"

He always called Nanny 'Mum', even though Ada kept correcting him. "She always does stuff like that," he said, and they carried on opening her presents and describing them. She'd asked for a pair of roller skates with flashing lights and, after Mum had put the eye cream on, her sticky eyes opened enough to see the flashy lights. They were great! She couldn't remember what her other presents were. There were almost too many of them and it was such a long time ago. Oh, except the strange naked little dolls with the legs that didn't move wrapped up together in a bundle of silky material and tied up with a fat gauzy ribbon and a label which said it was from Auntie Kira. "Typical Kira present, too," said Dad. Ada didn't remember Auntie Kira very well except that she smelled nice and had sewn a big X when her monkey had lost his eye so it always looked as if he had one eye tight shut now. She thought he was winking like Nanny. Just like they had a big secret. And maybe the secret was that real fairies don't wear sticky-out dresses.

Ada wasn't sure what to do with the dolls, so she tucked them into Nanny's box and put the box into the bottom drawer and, she remembered writing 'Pretty Old Things' on the lid.

She opened the box again. Yes, it was full of pretty things, except for some really ugly black buttons with long bits of thread on the back Ada guessed they were once sewn onto an old lady with a hat's big fat black coat. She'd never met the old lady with the hat, she was just 'imagining'. Ada thought all ladies in the olden days probably had hats. She thought 'Great Granny Ada' would have a hat that stuck to her head like the tiny ball of wool on one of the dolls she'd squashed in there on her birthday. There was a small pair of dark metal scissors inscribed 'Presented to Mrs Corcoran on the occasion of the launching of the Amy Howson'. Ada wondered who Mrs Corcoran was and who Amy Howson was. She remembered that Nanny had put the scissors in the box last time she visited just a few weeks ago, so she supposed that they must be friends of hers. Ada was allowed to use scissors at school and Mummy said she had to be careful because these scissors were pointy, but she couldn't resist a little snip across the gauze ribbon. Just to see how the scissors worked. Snip snip snip.

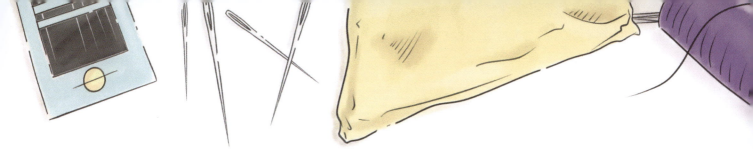

There was a little jumble of coloured threads all criss-crossing each other like a very wide plait, and a tiny blue packet like a long thin envelope printed in gold with a piece of black folded paper tucked into it… Inside the folded paper were some very shiny and very tiny sewing needles. Ada tried to take one out, but they all tumbled to the floor and stuck like spears into the carpet. Putting them back was quite difficult because the points kept pricking her fingers and the upside down ones just wanted to stick further into the carpet. The black paper kept wanting to fold back up, but there was something really satisfying about lining them all up again in a neat line and tucking them back into their teeny black bed. There was a twisted little creamy coloured paper bag with faded letters on it. It said 'Mrs Dry the Draper, and inside, folded into a multiple bow shape with the end wrapped several times round the middle and tucked inside itself, was a length of very narrow lilac-coloured ribbon.

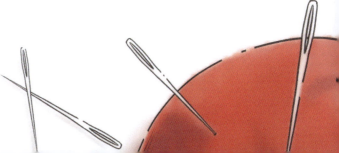

Nestled in the corner of the box was a funny little brown thing that looked like an egg in an egg cup and Ada fiddled with it for a few moments. It felt like the top was falling off and for a moment Ada worried in case Nanny might not like it if she broke it. Really carefully she tried pushing it, but it wouldn't push and it still felt wobbly. It twisted a bit though…and then it twisted right off! Inside was a silver thing that looked like a tiny drinking cup for a doll. It was covered in little dents as if someone had tried to make it look very old, but it was shiny like new and so Ada gave her monkey a drink of water out of it. Then she popped it on the end of her finger and twizzled it about while she emptied the rest of the box on the floor. It was crammed with buttons and ribbons and sparkly bits of broken jewellery and old-fashioned fasteners that looked like little hooks with curly edges, and other curly bits all sewn onto cardboard strips, and some things she'd seen in Nanny's house that Nanny called 'poppers' that closed together and opened with a satisfying click.

There was also a wheel made from a long ribbon that had numbers on it. It was for measuring. Nanny was singing a song about caterpillars that measured flowers while she rolled it up into a wheel and put a pin through it on the same day she'd given her the scissors. Ada pulled the pin out and unrolled it. She made it move like the caterpillar Nanny had called it an 'inch worm'. Then she rolled it all up tightly and put the pin back in. It was difficult to push the pin right into the wheel, so she pushed it with the silver cup.

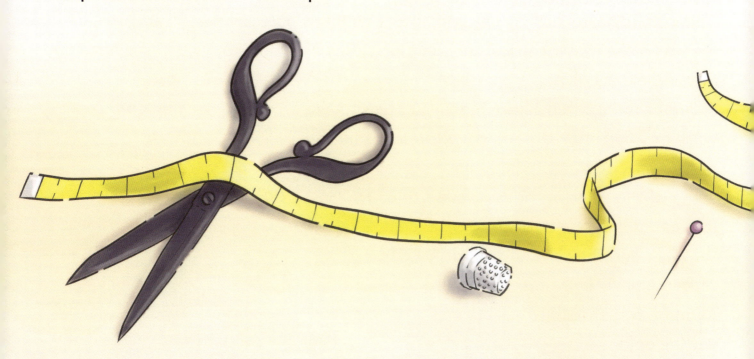

Jammed right in the very bottom of the box was a big torn envelope with a picture of an old-fashioned lady in a dress with sequins on and a feather in her short hair. Ada carefully teased the envelope out of the box, but it kept tearing and the pretty lady's legs came right off just under the knees. She looked like a short lady with a long dress now. Inside the envelope was a big wad of very thin, pale-brown tracing paper.

Ada took out the pieces one by one and smoothed them on to the floor of her bedroom. She started drawing fairies on them with her felt-tip pens. Then she saw that the pieces were funny shapes like a jigsaw and she put the long bits side by side and saw that they were like pieces of a dress, a bit like the one on the envelope. Ada laid on her back and then on her front full length on the paper and then gathered it all together around her waist and imagined she had a dress made of rustling paper all tied up with string.

Then Mum started calling her and so she shouted "just a minute!" and quickly folded up the jigsaw papers, but she found they wouldn't go back in the envelope or the box any more.

Ada quickly counted all the buttons back into the box. She decided counting wasn't so bad after all. Some button cards had six of the same sort, some had four or three; and some of the prettiest ones just had one. She lost count and stuffed everything except the dolls and the silk and the wispy crispy ribbon quickly back into the box as Mummy was shouting that tea was getting cold.

But tea was cold anyway because it was salad. Why did adults always say 'Your tea's getting cold' or 'dinner's in the dog' when none of that was true. Mummy had made almond cake for afters. "Nanny's favourite," she said, and Ada did like it too. Mummy made the best cakes! But today all Ada could think about were the poor little dolls with no clothes on.

"Mummy," Ada said with a mouth full of 'the sort of salad little girls like', as Nanny always called food when Ada wasn't sure if she was going to like something. Nanny wasn't a good cook, not like Mummy and Grandma, so she always made jokes that weren't funny about food.

"Mmmm ... Mum, did you ever sew?" "Not really," said Mum. "I'm so busy at work that it's not worth it and Grandma will sew buttons on. Nanny used to sew a bit.

Daddy once told me she made him a suit that looked like a rap singer's outfit". Ada chuckled, although she wasn't sure what a rap singer's outfit was, but Mummy thought it was funny so she knew it must be. She already knew Nanny could sew because of the ladybird story and because she'd seen her sewing machine and she'd shown Ada how to thread a needle with a little wire loop.

"And what about the one Nanny calls Nanny when she's talking to Dad? " Ada asked between mouthfuls. But Mum was busy clearing up the pots and told her she'd have to ask Dad when he got home.

"You can play in your room 'til then if you like".

This suited Ada just fine, as she had a very important job to do before bedtime, and she skipped up the stairs two at a time.

"It's way past your bedtime," said Dad, indulgently, as he tucked Ada up for the night. "Shall I read you the one about Matilda?" But Ada was more interested in answers to the questions that had been on her mind all day. "And did Nanny's mummy sew too?" "Well…" Daddy always started a sentence with 'well' when he was trying to remember stuff. "Well, she made me some shirts when I was a little boy. I think all the women in my family sewed. Maybe even all the way back… probably to Great Ada." He'd also slipped into the habit of calling Ada's great-four-times-grandma 'Great'. She must have sewed a bit because you have her button box. But I couldn't possibly know if she sewed a lot or just mended things, because she died a long, long time ago." "Night, night, Adapants! Sweet dreams." And Ada snuggled down to dream of fairies and dragonflies.

'But I do know,' mused Ada out loud as she fell asleep cuddled up with her three little dolls, each one wrapped carefully in a different coloured piece of silk, tied round with a lilac ribbon waistband with a bow and tiny flower tucked into each. And each now had a pair of gauzy wings on their backs. Attached with one simple cross stitch.

Biographies

Author Angie Scarr is better known as a best-selling miniature craft and craft-business writer, Angie and her husband and publishing-partner Frank live in an inland village in Andalusia Spain where Angie continues to grow old as disgracefully as possible.

Her Ada stories are based on the brief but delightful times she spends with her grandchildren and on events from her own childhood.

Illustrator Scott Macniven lives in Australia with his wife, two daughters, and incredibly daffy dog named Indy. He is an international fantasy artist with many works selling in galleries, and loves to enjoy a fun, whimsical, and artistic time with his family.

Printed in Great Britain
by Amazon